O My Days

a play by Dana Schwartz
based on the Novel
by David Mathew

MONTAG

A Montag Press Book
www.montagpress.com
Montag Press
777 Morton Street, Unit B
San Francisco CA 94129 USA

Montag Press, the burning book with the hatchet cover, the skewed word mark and the portrayal of the long-suffering fireman mascot are trademarks of Montag Press.

Printed & Digitally Originated in the United States of America
10 9 8 7 6 5 4 3 2 1

Settings:

Various locations inside Dellacotte Young Offenders Penitentiary:

> Cooking Class
>
> Library
>
> Cells
>
> Yard
>
> Puppydog Ward
>
> Visitor's Ward
>
> Hospital

Prison Ship

Oasis

Character Breakdown:

Billy Alfreth	-	early 20's, inmate, cocky, confused
Ronald Dott	-	20's, inmate, evil
Ostrich	-	20's, inmate, cool, sensitive *
Kate Thistle	-	30's, educated, kind, curious
Roller	-	20's, inmate, more brawn than brain *
Female	-	plays multiple characters, including Guard, Inmate, Mum
Male	-	plays multiple characters, including Guard, Inmate, Victim

* Ostrich and Roller can double with Guards and Inmates as needed

Note on casting. These are modern day people, diverse in race and size and socio-economic background. Casting should be diverse as well.

Acknowledgements:

Playwright would like to thank David Mathew for the novel and the wonderfully complex characters he created. Also thanks to Charlie Franco and everyone at Montag Press for their continual support.

Synopsis:

Incarcerated for a crime he definitely did commit, Billy Alfreth is trying to serve his sentence in peace. His world starts to unravel when Kate Thistle arrives, ostensibly to do prison research, but actually to research Billy himself. She's also got an interest in Ronald Dott, a new prisoner, but all together too familiar for Billy's comfort. Caught between realities, Billy must try to discover how their lives all connect in Time, while doing Time.

Bio:

DANA SCHWARTZ is a writer, director, actress working in her adopted home of Los Angeles for the past couple of decades. Her full length play "Early Birds" had its World Premiere at the Atwater Village Theater in 2019. Her play "@Playaz" is a 2019 O'Neill Finalist. "Perspective" recently enjoyed its World Premiere at Theater at the Museum at LACMA. "The PTA" and "That Time She Proposed" were in several productions of the internationally renowned Car Plays, notably at REDcat LA, Disney Hall, Segerstrom Arts and Costa Mesa. "Undead" will be produced at Theater Roulette in Cleveland, and "Epitaph" is her first published play. She is the co-creator and Producer of Theater at the Museum at LACMA, and is currently the Producer of the MADlab New Play Development Program at Moving Arts, where she is also a company member.

Scene 1

Cooking Class

ROLLER, INMATE 2, OSTRICH & BILLY are at stations, watching a GUARD demo making a recipe, as they follow along. Music plays under, and the lesson looks like a dance. They are in sync, flowing. They pour, they mix, they taste. Suddenly, ROLLER moves out of sync and rushes at TWO, grabs him and begins to beat him. The sound of the fight is discordant to the cooking rhythm and jars the rest of the class out of their dreamlike trance. It is chaos. Alarms ring, lights flash, smoke begins to rise from the cooking stations. Shouting, yelling, laughing.

Time starts to stretch. The sounds start to slow, like a record played at the wrong speed. The movement, while keeping its intensity, slows as well. This happens mid- fight, holds for a moment, then back to regular speed.

GUARD TWO rushes in, pulls ROLLER off of INMATE TWO. The INMATES don't resist, but the GUARDS beat them down anyway. ROLLER and TWO lie side by side on the ground.

Time stretches again.

The two GUARDS lean down and kiss the INMATES as they lay prone on the floor.

Time returns to regular speed.

BILLY

O my days!

INMATES

O my days!

End Scene 1

Scene 2

Prison yard.

OSTRICH is smoking a
cigarette.

BILLY enters

BILLY

Ay Ostrich.

OSTRICH

Wogwon Billy Alfreth. Come an sit for a bit.

BILLY

What are you doing out here bruv? It's cold.

OSTRICH

Why not. Man live in a box, man want to be unwrapped, time
to time.

BILLY

Allow it.

OSTRICH

Big Man jail, man go out whenever he wants. Blessed.

BILLY

Big Man jail's tough. This here is sick.

OSTRICH

Nah Billy. This here? This is explosive.

pause

BILLY gestures to the cigarette

                    BILLY

Twos on your burn?

                              OSTRICH hands it to him for
                              a drag

                    OSTRICH

Man been earning this month, get you a whole pack a burn.

                    BILLY

Friday. Bash mag too.

                              They smoke in friendly silence
                              for a beat.

                    BILLY (con't)

What you make of this morning? In Cookery.

                    OSTRICH

Which part Man?

                    BILLY

It was all off, wasn't it.

                    OSTRICH

Allow it.

                    BILLY

The time thing. It was put on peculiar.

                    OSTRICH

Time went... long.

                    BILLY

Yes!

                    OSTRICH

Time went devious.

4

BILLY

Exactly. Devious.

> GUARDS enter with DOTT.
> They are fully armed, he is in
> chains. He is trouble. They
> walk him slowly across.

OSTRICH

Who that?

BILLY

Heard his name is Dott. Ronald. He's thenew fish.

OSTRICH

HE the fish? He's the size of a poodle!

BILLY

Fourteen women, bruv. Man Life-ed off.

OSTRICH

I shoulda never stopped at four. Just breaking cherry.

BILLY

What are you talking about? Your bird ain't long enough for
the four you did?

OSTRICH

whispering

There's three more no man know about, Billy.

> DOTT and GUARDS pass, and
> DOTT stops directly in front of
> BILLY. DOTT stares.

BILLY

Ay. Fuck off then.

OSTRICH

Watch it bruv. You lose that Redband.

BILLY

Man got to know he can't just stare.

GUARD

Let's move Fish!

BILLY

You heard 'em. Move along.

DOTT

I'll be seeing you around. Billy.

GUARDS drag DOTT off.

End Scene 2.

Scene 3

In silhouette is a morning in
Prison. Doors clanking, a bell
rings. A club hitting the bars of
a cell.

GUARD

Alfreth?

BILLY

Gov?

GUARD

You showering this morning?

BILLY

No sir.

GUARD

You filthy, boy?

BILLY

No sir, saving my shower entitlement for the weekend.

GUARD

Get ready for work then. Redbands report in twenty.

BILLY

Yes sir!

We hear another bell, and the
cell doors slide open. Sound of
feet.

Library.

                        KATE THISTLE is seated as
                        BILLY enters.

                    KATE

Mr. Alfreth?

                    BILLY

Yes, Miss.

                    KATE

Hello. My name is Miss Thistle. Kate. I'm writing a disserta-
tion about the Young Offenders experience for my PhD. I've
chosen Dellacotte to start. They offered me a desk here in the
Library. I trust I won't be disturbing you.

                    BILLY

Thistle? You seem more like a Rose than a -

                    KATE

Alfreth. That's a Derbyshire name, isn't it?

                    BILLY

Innit.

                    KATE

It is indeed. A town I think. Maybe a village.

                    BILLY

Never seen it.

                    KATE

Well.

                        an awkward silence

                    BILLY

Well. Better get wriggling then. Orders to fill, whatnot.

KATE

Mr. Alfreth, I work for the University. That's why they've
allowed me to be - that's why I'm here. I want to know about
Learning Pathways for Young Offenders. Not just facts. Stats.
What have you. I can read about those in reports. I'm inter-
ested in, well, in your experience. Here in the Education
Department.

BILLY

You want a guinea pig.

KATE

Not exactly.

BILLY

You want a snitch?

KATE

No.

BILLY

I don't snitch.

KATE

I don't require a snitch.

BILLY

Come again?

KATE

I require a mind.

BILLY

I can't believe they let a - someone like you, in a place like
this. Aren't you afraid you'll get mashed? This is a Maximum
Security Prison, not a bleeding Uni.

KATE

Mr. Alfreth - may I call you by your first name?

BILLY

You don't know my first name.

KATE

It's William.

a beat

BILLY

Well. Usually it's Billy.

KATE

Billy it is then. Billy, I'm going to be here for a while. On a placement. Do you know what that is?

BILLY gives her a look

KATE (con't)

Yes. Well, I requested to work with someone with -intelligence. An Enhanced Level prisoner who knows the workings of the Education Department here inside and out. They gave me you, Billy.

BILLY

Still sounds like a snitch gig to me Miss Thistle.

KATE

Please, call me Kate.

BILLY

Oh.

KATE

What happened here yesterday. In the Cookery class? You were there?

BILLY

Ay.

KATE

It sounds like it was quite... intense.

BILLY

Ay.

KATE

You don't have to talk to me about it. I just assumed you
might know -

BILLY

No, I dunno. Can't really remember I guess. Yoots what
started it are in solitary. Screws are gone home. Must have
been something. I dunno.

KATE

I see. No conflict between them prior?

BILLY

No Miss. Shit went long in a hot minute.

KATE

I heard you say that to the Governor. I sat in on some of the
Adjudication this morning. I'm asking you privately now, what
happened.

BILLY

Like I said.

KATE

Cookery is a popular course.

BILLY

Ay. Best meal of the week.

KATE

So it's a privilege to be in there?

BILLY

Allow it.

KATE

I would assume that cuts down on the conflicts. In class.

BILLY

No one kicks off in Cookery Miss. Rudeboy what gets Cookery cancelled gets a right battering later. Or worse, the cold
shoulder.

KATE

There are consequences.

BILLY

Of course.

KATE

From the guards?

BILLY

Guards. D's. Yeah.

KATE

So why would they risk it?

BILLY

Like I says. I dunno.

KATE

You personally run a great risk if you are found to be lying
about this, don't you. Loss of privileges, Enhanced Status.
Quite a lot at stake for you.

BILLY

Not for nothing Miss, but what does this have to do with
Learning Pathways?

KATE

Sharp Billy. Very sharp. Ok then. Let's talk about you.

BILLY

What about me Miss?

KATE

Do you ever get - homesick? For your family? Parents?

BILLY

I miss my mum. I don't think many of us in here missing our
dads.

KATE

Do you regret yourmisdeed? The one that sent you here?

pause

BILLY

Allow it.

KATE

You don't have to tell me. But you can if you'd like.

BILLY

How old are you?

KATE

Tell me about your dreams Billy.

BILLY

Eh?

KATE

I sawin your file that you have trouble at night sometimes. Is that right? Trouble sleeping. Do you ever remember your dreams?

Lights shift.

BILLYis in his head.

BILLY

My life begins at night. Is that what you want to hear? Night brings the truth and my dreams are my salvation. Dreams are the only thing I have for myself anymore. The only thing I can call my own. In one, I'm back in Brixton and I do it all in reverse.

In silhouette, VICTIM appears. As if watching a tape in reverse, BILLY un-stabs his arm. Three times. VICTIM un-punches BILLY in the face. BILLY un-robs VICTIM, and hewalks backwards offstage.

BILLY (con't)

When I do it over, front-wise? I'm not mugging. Not high and looking for money. Looking for a fight. I'm showing him how to get to the museum or some such. No, not him. Them. There were three. Three of them, and I'm helping. And I'm vindi-cated. For what, I don't know, because I absolutely did it. Pled guilty and everything. It's just - sometimes I get the memory of it mangled with another. Where I'm the one being attacked. Fighting for my life. I can't - Ah, no matter. I love my dreams. Even the bad ones. Because reality is the horror, innit?

Lights shift back, BILLY turns back to KATE

BILLY (con't)
Just the usual. Arianna Grande sucking my dick. You know.

KATE
You don't have to put on for me Billy.

BILLY
Miss Thistle. Kate. You don't want to hear the truth about
this place. Masters level or no. You don't want to hear about
guards raping us in the night and playing it off as a cavity
search or whatnot. Don't want to hear about the yoot what
fucked a dog before he killed it. And then killed the family what owned it. It's sick here, Miss. Dark. You'll do well to
remember that. If you want to talk about Learning Whatsits,
that's all right. But mind what you ask about the rest. I'd hate
to be the one what scares you off.

PA system beeps.

P/A VOICE
Library Redband. Report to A Wing. Book deliveries may
commence.

BILLY
Sorry Miss, that's me.

KATE
You better go then. We'll talk more soon. Nice to meet you Billy.

She extends her hand to him.
He hesitates, takes it carefully.
BILLY grabs his big yellow
delivery bag full of reading
materials and starts to exits.

KATE (con't)
And so you know? I don't scare easy.

> BILLY looks at her for
> moment. He exits.

End Scene 3.

Scene 4

Prison Yard.

> OSTRICH and BILLY are smoking, one last one before bed.

BILLY

That was the first female flesh I touched in two years, four months and seventeen days. It was like stepping on the moon.

OSTRICH

Man fall in love for lesser ting.

BILLY

Allow it.

OSTRICH

What of Julie?

BILLY

It's over.

OSTRICH

Mother of your daughter Man.

BILLY

She's moved on. Said my Patrice needs a real Dad. Better off. Got my suspicions confirmed at least, it's easier this way.

OSTRICH

Rough.

BILLY

Man alive, I can't wait til the weekend.

OSTRICH

It IS the weekend Man.

BILLY

Tomorrow night I mean. Saturday. Playing Shelly at pool.
Three burn stake Man.

OSTRICH whistles, impressed.

OSTRICH

Who know about it?

BILLY

You me and him. I can trust you Ostrich, eh?

OSTRICH

Man lip as sealed as a lady panda poom-poom. But you
watch yourself. They catch you gambling again you lose that
Enhanced. There go your Miss Thistle then, what?

BILLY

He challenged me. Can't let it get around Man challenge me
and I don't do nothing about it.

OSTRICH

You just got your job. You fight, it's gone. Man need to contemplate the ifs.

BILLY

I won't lose to that fucking squirrel.

OSTRICH

Just contemplate.

BILLY

You know I'm right bruv. Man can't ignore a duel. Not in here.

OSTRICH

Allow it.

PA crackles

PA V/O

Lights out in five minutes. Lights out in five minutes. Inmates return to your cells immediately. Anyone caught out will be searched and reported.

OSTRICH

That's us then.

OSTRICH stubs out his cigarette and starts to go. BILLY stops him.

BILLY

Ostrich man?

OSTRICH

We gotta move Billy, let's go.

BILLY

Listen though. What I win tomorrow, yeah?

OSTRICH

Yeah?

BILLY

It's yours Ostrich. All three burn.

OSTRICH stops and turns to look at him.

BILLY (con't)

I need you to do something for me though.

OSTRICH

Time to go Billy.

BILLY

If you tell me about the others you killed. Three burn.

pause

OSTRICH

Seems important.

BILLY

Nah man. It's vital. That thing in Cookery. I know what I saw.
Now I need to know WHY I saw it. I have to know. I think - I
think this could be a start.

End Scene 4

Scene 5

Puppydog Wing.

A GUARD is at the entrance.

BILLY enters with his delivery bag.

GUARD

You're late.

BILLY

Ay sir.

GUARD

Might have to let these Puppydogs have their way with you.

BILLY

Well sir. Not up to me when I get released from Library now is it.

GUARD

Watch that tone.

BILLY

Sorry. Can I get on then?

GUARD

Hold your horses there a minute boy. You know the drill. What's in the bag?

BILLY

Ay sir. A New Scientist for Schyler. Book on Football for Downe. TV Guide for Dott.

GUARD

New fish. Getting his library order placed pretty fast. What's that about?

                    BILLY
Not my job to wonder sir. Just here to honor my duty to dispatch.

                    GUARD
Well. Bugger off then.

                    BILLY
Allow it.

                    GUARD
I'll allow it when you're dead, Alfreth.

                    BILLY
Rough morning sir? You seem -

                    GUARD
Start your rounds.

                              BILLY stands for a moment,
                              about to say more.

                              GUARD bangs his club hard on
                              the wall.

                    GUARD (con't)
I said START YOUR ROUNDS.

                    BILLY
Thank you sir.

                              BILLY begins his deliveries.
                              He walks to a cell, bangs on
                              the door, and tosses the deliv-
                              ery down. This should have
                              a rhythm to it, with the door
                              bangs and mail drops becom-
                              ing a percussive song. BILLY

                    22

> savors this freedom of move-
> ment. After a few moments, the
> rhythm is broken with -

DOTT

Hey Library!

> BILLY is startled, only for a
> slight second, then heads to
> Dott's Cell.

> He bangs the door and tosses
> the delivery, but his rhythm is
> off.

BILLY

TV Guide.

> DOTT enters, close to the door.

DOTT

What happened to them Screws?

BILLY

Come again?

DOTT

The two Screws from Cookery Room.

BILLY

How do you know about that?

DOTT

News travels swift.

BILLY

I guess so.

DOTT

Suspended? Fired?

BILLY

I don't even know, really.

DOTT

Do me a favor? Keep me posted?

BILLY

Why would I go an do a thing like that, eh?

DOTT

Oh Billy. I can treat you in SO many ways.

BILLY

Fuck off, perv. You threatening me?

DOTT

Not at all Billy. It's a promise. A very good one at that.

BILLY

How the hell do you know my name?

DOTT

Ah Billy. Don't you know? I can hear your whispers. I can see your dreams.

> Lights shift and DOTT's is in
> Billy's head

DOTT V/O

Give my love to pretty Kate Thistle.

> BILLY grabs his headas DOTT
> laughs

End Scene 5

Scene 6

Library.

KATE and BILLY are working

KATE

I haven't had the pleasure.

BILLY

Ay. Plus, he's a baby faced wanker. It's odd.

KATE

Why is that odd?

BILLY

Well, typically Miss? If a bruv is in here and he has that baby face, it ain't because of good genetics, if you know what I mean.

KATE

I don't think I do.

BILLY

Dott's not wrinkled 'cause he ain't got cares. He ain't been roughed up by his - thoughts? He just don't give a f-

KATE

Billy.

BILLY

He ain't got no remorse is what I mean.

KATE

I see.

BILLY

Got them other freaks on his block worked up, that's for sure.

KATE

He just got here.

BILLY

One yoot offered me a pouch of burn to have him - talked to.

KATE

Talked to. You mean roughed up, don't you?

BILLY

No Miss.

KATE

You're a terrible liar Billy.

BILLY smiles.

KATE (con't)

Is a "pouch of burn" a lot?

BILLY

Ay Miss. Never known a stake so high.

KATE

Interesting.

BILLY

Allow it.

KATE

You turned it down.

BILLY

Of course!

KATE smiles.

> BILLY (con't)

Nice that he thought I could manage it though. Not that I would risk my Redband for that wank. But nice to be remembered, you know?

> KATE

It's the little things.

> BILLY

You have no idea Miss.

> pause

> KATE

Something's on your mind.

> BILLY

Been wondering. Why would you choose to come here? Not one of US wants to be here, yet here you are.

> KATE

May I ask you something?

> BILLY

Ay.

> KATE

Do you ever think about your past?

> pause

> BILLY

Nope.

> KATE

Really?

> BILLY

Naw Miss. I never think about it 'cause I ain't got one.

                    KATE

Everyone has a past.

                    BILLY shrugs

                    KATE (con't)

Don't you ever think about your crimes?

                    BILLY

Nope

                    KATE

Why not?

                    BILLY

Virgin.

                    KATE

Excuse me?

                    BILLY

I'm innocent Miss.

                    KATE

The judge didn't seem to think so.

                    BILLY

Judge didn't have three coked up yoots tryin' to kick his eyes
out, now did he?

                    KATE

Billy.

                    BILLY

It were self defense.

                    KATE

Your file says there was only one man there.

                        BILLY

Three men.

                        KATE

I've seen the film. CCTV.

                        BILLY

Me too, but there was three -

                    Lights shift. BILLY's head

                    BILLY (con't)

I was attacked by three men that night. I know this in my
bones. Three. But then, I get... confused? Sometimes. I have
been in a situation where I was attacked by three men, I know
I have, but I can't... recall. Exactly. The details? What they
have me on however, is an attack I made on one guy. The only
thing I ever been caught for...

                    Lights shift back.

                    BILLY (con't)

You been studying up on me then?

                        KATE

I told you. My business is research.

                        BILLY

Lots more interesting things to research around here Miss.

                        KATE

What did you talk to Dott about?

                        BILLY

Who says I talked to him? Just dropped off his order is all.

KATE

You were at his cell door for quite a while.

BILLY

No privacy in this shit hole.

KATE

Did you want privacy?

BILLY

Fuck no!

KATE

Billy.

BILLY

Sorry miss. But no. Why would I want privacy with the likes of that raping piece of shit?

KATE

I wondered the same thing.

BILLY

What do you care?

pause

KATE

Research.

BILLY

Sounds like something a copper would ask, Miss.

KATE

Are you married Billy?

BILLY

What?

                    KATE

You have a daughter, yes?

                    BILLY

Allow it.

                    KATE

How is that going?

                         Lights shift, BILLY's head

                    BILLY V/O

Let me talk to her!

                    JULIE V/O

She's upstairs with the babysitter. He's putting her down for
her -

                    BILLY V/O

He?!

                    JULIE V/O

She needs a father Billy!

                         Lights shift back

                    BILLY

About how you'd expect.

                    KATE

You talk?

                    BILLY

Sure. But what is there to say when you said it all last week.
And the week before that.

                    KATE

That must be hard.

BILLY

Easier now. She's replaced me.

KATE

I'm sorry to hear.

BILLY

Allow it. Better for everyone.

End Scene 6

Scene 7

Prison Yard.

> BILLY is there. OSTRICH
> enters.

OSTRICH

Wogwon Billy.

BILLY

You save it?

> OSTRICH pulls a sandwich out
> of his shirt with a flourish

OSTRICH

Ta da! And yourself then?

> BILLY produces his own
> sandwich

BILLY

It's like going out for dinner.

OSTRICH

I'm your date!

BILLY

We're an item!

> They laugh, eat. Their silence
> is comfortable, easy.

After a moment, BILLY looks
around the yard, making sure
no one is watching, and pulls
out three cigarettes. He offers
them to OSTRICH. He hesi-
tates, and then reluctantly takes
them and hides them away.

OSTRICH

You sure you wanna hear this Man?

BILLY

I'm sure.

OSTRICH

Ah Billy, man, I don't understand why you need to - you know
what, all right. A deal is deal, what? So. What do you want to
know?

BILLY

About the others you did. Tell me.

OSTRICH sighs and preps himself to tell it

OSTRICH

You know when you have to do something. Regardless of the
consequences?

BILLY

We're all here for precisely that reason Man.

OSTRICH

Nah man. I ain't talking about normal crime-madness.

BILLY

What are you chatting?

OSTRICH

We're criminals, blood.

BILLY

Allow it.

OSTRICH

Are you listening though? We made choices. We took
chances. We gamble. But we didn't HAVE to do it. Right? We
might have come into some beef. Lost some face, maybe. But
we didn't have to do it bruv.

BILLY

Swear down.

OSTRICH

So imagine a situation. A thing where you know the conse-
quence be deep, blood. But you absolutely HAVE to do it.
There's no freewill about the madness.

BILLY

Are you talking a family thing?

OSTRICH

Yeah. Yeah. Straight down, confrontation, mad astronaut shit
family thing.

BILLY

That's the shit.

OSTRICH

Allow it. But this is lips-is-sealed, right?

BILLY

I'm surprised you have to ask.

OSTRICH

Yeah. Check it.

They fist bump

OSTRICH (con't)

It was a thing with my Mum. Gets herself a new man. And he all right. She had a few before, O my Days. Just there to take up space, bruv.

BILLY

Sounds familiar.

OSTRICH

This one was okay. Anthony. Gave me stodge about staying out too late. 'You have to go to school!' All like that. 'You're disappointing me'. Yeah, he was okay. I was preparing his Father's Day present. Out there, all hours, jacking cars and stereos and shit, get some money to buy Man a nice gift. Show my respect. I go to bare trouble, bruv. Get him a nice set of cufflinks. Cost me bare peas, blood! And what does that waste do? He go and leave my Mumsy on Father's Day!

BILLY

Fucker!

OSTRICH

Mum is ruined. Obliterated. So I'm in the market for buying up a nine-millimeter strap and putting a hole in his heard. But Mumsy's all "no, no, don't do it!" Why not? I know where he lives. Won't take long.

BILLY

It's what any good son would do, blood.

OSTRICH

Allow it. So I dust over to his house. Driving a 2-liter whip in them days.

BILLY

With a strap?

OSTRICH

Nah man, just going to polish the man's face. Seeing Mumsy
on the vodka at ten in the damn morning. I wasn't going to
stand for that, no way. She gives me a toot on my mobile.
"Don't do it Maxwell. I'm begging you. Don't do it!" And I'm
like "why Ma?" and that's when she drops her fucking bomb-
shell. "He's your Dad, Maxwell."

BILLY

O my days.

OSTRICH

Yeah man. My own dad leave my own mum on fucking
Father's Day. Unbelievable.

BILLY

Youknock him out?

OSTRICH

Eventually. But I find out what the game is first. I learn that
Father's Day is not exclusive to me. Man has other yoots. So
I ring his bell, Man comes out, saying "yeah, sorry, shit didn't
work out," and I say "Anthony? It's Father's Day and I want
to give you a present." And BAM! Five knuckles to his chin.
The waste drops. And I look up and who's there? Babymama
three, with her yoot. And fucking Babymama two, who happens to be cousins, and I'm rah. What's a man to do? I go in
knowing and there's no way of going out, innit.

BILLY

You killed the Babymanas?

OSTRICH

No man! A course not. Point I'm making here is, I have no
choice. This was family, bruv. Ignoring it was not an option.
It's got nothing to do with Mum. It's me.

pause

BILLY

He hit his head on the way down. Didn't he.

OSTRICH

Little table with the phone on it. A chance in a fucking million. Damage his neurons. I kill my own dad.

BILLY

That's tough Ostrich. I'm sorry, bruv.

OSTRICH

I ain't finished, Rudeboy. So I dust the fuck out of there.
Babymamas ain't seen shit. I'm a free man. Conscience
excepted, of course.

BILLY

Allow it.

OSTRICH

Didn't realize tho. Man's new Daddy has siblings. Uncles. They
come around to my yard, explosive. I had to do some mad shit,
Rudeboy. Squash out three men. Happy Father's Day.

BILLY

The third one you got caught?

pause

                    OSTRICH
That's the deal.

                    BILLY
You swear?

                    OSTRICH
Swear bruv.

                    Light shift, BILLY's head.

                    BILLY
Is it about killing? Revenge? Violence. The story isn't helping.
I feel like I almost understand, I almost get it, but then it slips
away like a dream.

                    Lights shift back.

                    OSTRICH
Oh. You hear the word?

                    BILLY
What word?

                    OSTRICH
Mobile found. Some yoot keep it secluded up his ass on a
piece of cord. For four months! Screw tells him to squat gives
the cord a playful yank. Apparently, man's screams could be
heard from A Wing to the Workshop.

                    BILLY
Heinous.

                    OSTRICH
What if it rang inside his intestine?

BILLY

Hello? It's for you!

OSTRICH

Sorry bruv, can't come to the phone right now!

They laugh.

End Scene 7.

Scene 8

Puppydog Ward. Dott's cell.

BILLY drops the delivery and
bangs on the door. He starts to
turn away

DOTT

Took you long enough.

BILLY

Never in a hurry to come to Puppydog.

DOTT

What time is it Billy?

BILLY

About ten I reckon.

DOTT

It's ten-fourteen. And 32, 33, 34 seconds.

BILLY

Why the fuck did you ask me then, dickhead?

He starts to go

DOTT

Oh Billy?

BILLY

What do you want?

DOTT

I have a message. For Kate Thistle. If you don't mind? Tell
her, Don't try it. Tell her, She's nowhere near as smart as she

thinks. That I've left smarter women than her in a city car park, bleeding internally and wondering what the hell they've done to deserve me.

Lights shift. BILLY's head

BILLY

Alarms going off. Fear like bile rising up into my mouth. I can't let him see he's getting to me. Can't let him see weakness. It's like that documentary they made us watch, where the baby alligator swallows a deer. I'm the fucking deer.

Lights shift

BILLY

The fuck you talking about?

DOTT

Her silly mind games. They won't work.

pause

BILLY

I'll tell her. If you tell me what you mean.

DOTT

Kate Thistle knows what I mean. Do you know a bee can only sting once before it dies?

BILLY

I - uh - yeah, I heard that.

DOTT

Unlucky for the bee. Wasps though? Sting and sting and sting.

BILLY

What you been smoking man?

DOTT

I'm the wasp Billy. You're the bee. Forget about the alligators
and deer. You've got bigger things to worry about. So does
your Miss Thistle if she's not careful. Tell her. TELL HER!

> BILLY looks straight out at the
> audience as alarm bells ring.
> BILLY walks quickly away as
> we hear DOTT screaming and
> GUARD yelling as lights shift

GUARD

Shut the fuck up Dott, don't make me come in there!

> DOTT screams, cell clangs, we
> hear a crash!

End Scene 8

Scene 9

Library

> KATE is working. BILLY rushes
> in, sees that she's alright. Takes
> a breath. Lights shift to BILLY's
> Head.

BILLY

How did he read my mind? Did I give something away? I
don't like to give nothing away. Nothing is free. I want to tell
her, be careful. I want to tell her, he knows about you. Why
do I feel like she already knows? I want to tell her about my
latest dream. Dott and I, sailing endless waters. I am Cap-
tain of a voyage that feels like pain. The waters drain and
we are sailing through a graveyard. As the ship ploughs the
land, the ghosts rise up like gusts of mist. They are prison-
ers. They dance. "Why have you found me?" I ask the ghosts.
"Because. We've finally done our time Billy." Dott is not sailing with me anymore. Dott is the ship. I want to tell her. But
I don't like to give nothing away.

> Lights shift back.

KATE

Hello! I thought you were on deliveries?

BILLY

Ay. Finished quick.

KATE

Lovely. What's the good word.

BILLY

Same same Miss.

KATE

No news?

BILLY

Nah. Nothing new.

pause

KATE

And, what's the word about me?

BILLY

Miss?

KATE

I've been here a good few weeks now. I know how you fellows talk among yourselves -

BILLY laughs

KATE (con't)

What?

BILLY

Nothing. I just ain't heard "fellows" in a time.

KATE

That's not true! The guards say it every day.

BILLY

One, Miss, it's officers not guards. And Two, it's "Fellas". Not "Fellows". Say "Fellows" in here, mocking is the least you'll get!

KATE

Thanks for the tip.

> BILLY looks at her for a moment.

BILLY

Trade down.

KATE

What do you propose?

BILLY

I'll tell you what they're saying about you. If you'll tell me why you're studying Dott.

> KATE looks at him for a moment.

KATE

I don't know what you mean.

BILLY

With respect, Miss. I think you might. He certainly knows you.

> pause

KATE

You first.

BILLY

We think you're a Fed.

> GUARD enters.

GUARD

What are you doing back here Alfreth?

BILLY

Finished my rounds Sir.

GUARD

Everything all right Miss?

KATE

Of course.

GUARD

Here you go Alfreth. Yootfrom IT Class needs to use the PC.
Driving test theory or some shit. You make sure it's not porn.

> GUARD shoves ROLLER in.

GUARD (con't)

You've got 30 minutes fellas. Miss? You want to come with me?
You have a call in the main.

KATE

Of course. Thank you Officer.

> KATE glances at ROLLER and
> BILLY. BILLY nods his head.
> KATE and GUARD exit.

BILLY

Wogwon Roller.

ROLLER

Wogwon Billy.

BILLY

You got my note.

ROLLER

Ay. Flushed it.

BILLY

Good.

ROLLER

Where's my burn then?

BILLY hands him a cigarette.

ROLLER

You said two.

BILLY

I'll owe you the other.

ROLLER

Allow it.

BILLY

So spill it. Quick. What really happened? Not the story you told in Adjudication. The real story.

ROLLER hesitates. Fingers the cigarette. Looks around.

ROLLER

Billy. I don't know. How to tell it. It was like... time stopped. I went dead. DEAD, man. Then - ay, I can't believe I'm - ok. There was someone else in my head. I could feel him in there, but I couldn't get him out. He tells me - he tells me he can make my time go faster. He's got a way. He shows me he - he can control people's minds. Some people. He makes me fuck Meaney up bad. I didn't want to, yoot done nothing, you know. Then. Then, he makes them screws kiss us. Just to fuck with us. Because he can. Man, I hated having him in my head Billy. He's evil.

BILLY

Dott.

ROLLER

They just took him to Segregation for two weeks. Fucked up a
Screw's cheekbone. With his toilet seat. Right after you left his
cell I heard. Maybe we'll get some peace.

BILLY

Maybe.

ROLLER

Want to know something else? That screw? What kissed me?
We're from the same ends.

BILLY

So what.

ROLLER

Them's bad ends, blood. How does a man from our ends end
up as a fucking screw? Most of us is more about not getting
blazed with a nine-millimeter, know what I mean?

BILLY

Coincidence.

ROLLER

Ay? Same ends as fucking Meany too, cuz.

BILLY

Meany's from the South Coast.

ROLLER

Grew up on the South Coast. Spent the last five years in
my ends. OUR ends Billy. Here's how I see it. Crime has its
neighborhoods, neighborhoods don't have crime. Know what
I mean? Crime chooses us. Because we lived in its ends.

BILLY

Maybe he's drugging us somehow. Or, oh! Mass hysteria, like that. Mass...misdirection.

ROLLER

That'd be a neat trick. Little rudeboy like that?

BILLY

History tells it, bruv. Man got a whole nation to believe in his murderous campaign. Cult leaders, whatnot. People can be manipulated. Happens all the time.

ROLLER

I don't like being manipulated. Feel like a puppet.

BILLY

Ay. But you have to applaud the show.

ROLLER

He's evil bruv. Watch yourself, digging around. Trust me, you don't want that blood in your head.

BILLY

Ay. But I gotta know. You know? I'm sorry for this Roller, really I am.

> BILLY punches ROLLER. As the lights fade we hear alarm bells and guards yelling.
>
> **End Scene 9.**

Scene 10

Segregation Unit.

The cells are tight, claustrophobic. DOTT is in his cell,

BILLY is led by GUARD.

GUARD

Welcome to Segregation Unit, wanker.

DOTT

Thank you for coming to see me darling!

GUARD

Fuck off Dott.

DOTT

You fancy going out tonight or shall we stay in?

GUARD

Shut the fuck up boy, don't make me tell you again!

BILLY

I'm sorry sir.

GUARD

For what?

BILLY

For having to listen to that from Dott. It was for my benefit.

GUARD

You two got beef?

BILLY

No, no, nothing serious.

DOTT

Only the night will say for sure!

> GUARD bangs on DOTT's
> door. He shoves BILLY into his
> cell, we hear the door slam.

GUARD

There better not be nothing. You hear me? Alright boy, you're
in Henry's cell. He made his escape using his pillow case as a
noose. Won't be seeing him again. Wonder if your friends are
thinking the same about you. Now keep your mouths shut you
two. You do not want to fuck around in Seg.

> GUARD bangs on DOTT's
> door one more time for good
> measure, exits.

> Lights shift. BILLY's head.

BILLY

What have I done? I've been to Seg before, sure, on Library
Business. But seeing it from the outside while I drop off a TV
Guide did not prepare me for this hell. I'm wet and hungry
and filled with a dread I can't explain. I hear the noises and
they are new and they are awful. Never have I heard young
men suffering so, O my days. But I'm obsessed now, I couldn't
stop this even if I wanted to. How has he done it? Not knowing is breaking my heart. I HAVE TO -

> Lights shift back.

BILLY (con't)

Dott!

pause

BILLY (con't)

DOTT!

GUARD V/O

Shut up immediately!

BILLY

Yes sir.

pause

BILLY (con't)

Dott. Can you hear me?

DOTT

I can always hear you, Billy. You don't ever have to yell.

BILLY

How?

DOTT

Wrong question.

BILLY

What then?

DOTT

What is your earliest memory of fear?

pause

BILLY

I was seven. Playing tag with my sisters. Got stung by a bee. My arm burned for a week, turns out I'm allergic.

DOTT

A million years of bee stings, Billy. Think about it.

BILLY

What the fuck you talking?

DOTT

You know Prometheus? He was -

BILLY

You insulting me now, bruv? I went to school, I -

DOTT

Tell me then.

BILLY

Prometheus stole fire from the gods. Gave it to the mortals.

DOTT

Very good. Be sure and read your visitor's message Billy.

BILLY

Don't talk in riddles, you fuck.

DOTT

Read it, and take heed.

BILLY

Who's my visitor?

no answer

BILLY (con't)

Who the fuck is it? Show me your hand! Show me your moth-erfucking currency, blood. You want me to believe in you? Show me!

DOTT

Who said I wanted you to believe anything?

DOTT laughs quietly

DOTT (con't)

It's your Mumsy, Billy.

BILLY

So much as touch her and I swear I'll make your life a living hell.

DOTT

What makes you think it isn't?

pause

DOTT (con't)

Here's my currency. Your first fear. When you were stung by the bee. I was there Billy. I was the one who poured water on the sting.

Lights shift, BILLY's head. A memory in shadow. A young boy is running, suddenly he grabs his arm and screams. He is dizzy, and falls to the ground, holding his arm and crying. A man appears, kneels next to the boy, and pours water on his arm. The boy stops crying. The

man brushes the boy's hair our
of his eyes. We hear the boy's
voice

BOY V/O

Thank you Ronald.

Lights shift back. BILLY falls
to the ground, exactly as the
shadow boy did.

GUARD enters, comes to
BILLY's cell.

GUARD

On your feet Alfreth, you lucky prick. You've got a visitor.

End Scene 10

Scene 11

Visitor's ward.

> GUARD in the corner. MUM
> sits at a table, BILLY enters.

BILLY

How the fuck do you know Ronald Dott, Mum?

MUM

Billy! You're not too old to be slapped you know? That's a fine way to greet his own Mother. I certainly didn't bring you up that way.

BILLY

Mum. Have you forgotten where you're visiting me?

> MUM looks away.

BILLY (con't)

I'm sorry.

MUM

Don't take that shitty tone with me, young man.

BILLY

Sorry.

> BILLY looks at her while call-
> ing to the GUARD

BILLY (con't)

Permission to hug my mum.

GUARD

Allow it.

>They have a perfunctory hug
>and sit.

MUM

Now. Who's this Reginald Dott?

BILLY

Ronald. You remember when I had that bee sting when I was seven or eight? There was a guy what lived downstairs.

MUM

You were seven.

BILLY

Seven then! There was a man downstairs.

MUM

Put water on it. I remember. Why do you ask?

BILLY

What was his name?

MUM

Goodness Billy, have you any idea how many people have been there?

BILLY

A lot, I know. But I thought you might remember something like that.

MUM

If you recall, I was more worried at that time about you needing spectacles.

BILLY

Spectacles?

MUM

It seemed like you weren't able to see the board at school.
BILLY sighs

BILLY

I know Mum. I was never there. I'm sorry. Again.

> She ignores him. This is an old
> game, they are experts.

BILLY (con't)

Mum. Mum? Could it have been Ronald?

MUM

I suppose it could have. What's up?

BILLY

But was it?

MUM

I don't know, baby boy!

> BILLY breathes deeply, regain-
> ing control

BILLY

Mum. What's the name at the bottom of the letter you've
been asked to bring me?

> MUM looks at him.

BILLY (con't)

May I see it?

MUM

It's unnamed. But it's not exactly a letter.

> BILLY calls to GUARD

59

BILLY

Permission to take a letter from Mumsy, sir?

> GUARD strolls over.

GUARD

Me first.

> He takes the letter and reads
> it. Slowly. Perhaps he moves his
> lips while he reads. BILLY tries
> not to show his frustration.

GUARD (con't)

What's all this then?

BILLY

It's a -

MUM

It's a work of fiction. From his sister. It's a story for her English class.

GUARD

"I can remember the first time he held me in his arms..."
Well. She's got talent I guess. But love stories aren't really my thing.

> GUARD tosses the letter to
> BILLY and strolls back to his
> corner.

BILLY

This came to the house?

MUM

I read as far as the request - "Search up 'Prometheus' and 'Hair Shirt'". I printed the results for you, love. That's as far as I read, I promise.

BILLY

Request?

> She hands him a few pages of printed copy.

MUM

Here's the information then. I typed directly from the screen. I knew I was part of your game Billy. Right or wrong, I knew.

BILLY

There's no game.

MUM

I didn't read any further, I swear. I knew the story bit was a disguise. I'm not stupid you know.

BILLY

I know.

MUM

Well.

> pause

BILLY

How's Julie then?

MUM

Shouldn't you know? Mother of your child.

BILLY

She fucking left me Mum.

MUM

Don't use that language in front of me.

BILLY

Sorry. Heard she's got a new bloke. What's he like?

MUM

I haven't met him. Why do you ask?

BILLY

Nothing.

MUM

That was always your father's answer as well.

BILLY

Ah Mum. What a grave disgrace I must truly be.

MUM

That's your words Billy, not mine. Better be off then, bus will be leaving.

> BILLY looks at her for a long moment.

BILLY

Permission to hug my mum.

GUARD

Allow it.

MUM

Allow it Billy.

> They embrace.

BILLY

Thank you Mumsy.

MUM

I'll send your best to your sisters. See you soon, love.

> MUM hugs him tightly once
> more, and leaves.

> BILLY stays at the table and
> reads the letter.

> Lights shift. BILLY's head

DOTT V/O

Billy. Forgive the four paragraphs of gobshite. Necessary work.
I'm sure you guessed the reason by now. Listen. Prometheus was
a cunning, deceitful piece of work. No awe for the gods. Ridi-
culed Zeus - that bastard god who denied man the secret of fire.
Prometheus felt pity for man, and stole the fire. Taught man to
cook. Zeus was so angry, he had an eagle peck at Prometheus's
liver for eons. Imagine that. What's the closest you can get to
that Billy? Incarceration? Fuck no. Imagine a million years of bee
stings. We got off lightly you and I. Well, you have at least. Even
the Greeks understood the liver is one of the only parts that can
regenerate itself. That's creative cruelty, that is. World War Two
cruelty. It's what I need but cannot find. By the time I'm free,
there will be nothing left but cockroaches. Wasps. Save me, Billy.
Help me like I helped you. I was there. It was me. You know it's
true. I used to think kindness was the key, but I was wrong. I'd be
closer to the end if I had slit your throat that day.I really wish I'd
smashed you up a bit when I had the chance. You have no idea
how much kindness has hindered me -

> GUARD has walked over and
> bangs his club against the table,
> startling BILLY out of his reverie.

GUARD

Enough of that now Alfreth! Back to Seg now. Lucky little shite, they're going to let you keep that Redband. For now. Let's move it along!

End Scene 11

Scene 12

Library.

> KATE is working, BILLY enters

KATE
Billy! How nice to see you.

BILLY
Thank you Miss.

KATE
You look well!

BILLY
Do I? I feel awful.

KATE
Was the Segregation Unit so bad?

BILLY
Like a million years of bee stings.

> KATE startles. BILLY watches
> her.

KATE
What a funny way to put it.

BILLY
Is it?

> pause

BILLY (con't)
You know Miss. I can make it all so much easier. Let me help you.

65

KATE

What makes you think you can help me.

BILLY

I know Dott. Or, I'm getting to know him.

KATE

And?

BILLY

You want to know him better. I might believe you're here for research, Kate. But you have nothing to do with education.

KATE

So why am I here.

BILLY

You're investigating the fact that Dott... doesn't seem to age. You're talking to people who knew him. Who have been affected by him.

pause

KATE

And that's you.

BILLY

And how come, by the way? How come you're allowed to be a non-prison employee and haveunescorted contact with an inmate?

KATE

Your records are exemplary Billy.

BILLY

Which you've read.

KATE

Of course.

BILLY

I can help you.

KATE

I know. I'm just not sure how to use you.

pause

BILLY

You could... use me to make tea.

KATE

Lovely. Brew up then.

BILLY makes tea

BILLY

So what's the arrangement?

KATE

I don't follow.

pause

BILLY

What do I get for helping you out?

KATE

What do you think I can give you?

BILLY

A meeting. With Dott.

KATE

I'm not sure I can swing that one around.

BILLY

You can if you want to.

pause

KATE

What about a visit. Would that do in the meantime?

BILLY

To where?

KATE

To his cell in the Seg. His TV magazine.

BILLY

Has he ordered one?

KATE

Yes. Normally it would go to his cell on the, what do you call
it? Puppydog Wing. Worth a try to get it into Segregation.

BILLY smiles

KATE (con't)

What's funny?

BILLY

Giving him a TV mag in a place where he's explicitly forbid-
den to watch TV. It's beautiful.

KATE

That's not quite what I had in mind.

BILLY

Miss, you don't have my mind.

KATE smiles

KATE

No. No, I don't. Not yet.

End Scene 12

Scene 13

Prison Yard

Inmates and Guards, the bustle
of morning. We hear bells
and clangs and shouting and
talking as people move though
the space. The P.A. speaker
crackles.

P.A.V/O
All inmates on the Labor List, report to Cookery. Repeat, all
inmates on Labor, report to Cookery. Class resumes today.

This is met with general good-
will. Shouts of excitement,
cheers, perhaps some boos.

OSTRICH and BILLY find
each other on the way to class.

OSTRICH
Back to Cookery, ay Billy?

BILLY
Let's not fuck it up. Get us a proper meal.

OSTRICH
You heard who else is in there then?

BILLY
Roller and Meaney. Together again.

OSTRICH

Ay. And Dott.

BILLY

Figures.

OSTRICH

Wogwan Billy? You all right?

BILLY

I'm all right fam.

OSTRICH

What be going on man?

BILLY

Complicated.

pause

OSTRICH

We trade, yeah? I spilled my beans for you. Now man creep
man some rumor in return.

BILLY

Go ahead, blood. Might help. Coming back from Seg is like
returning from a foreign country. Feel like I been stalled at
Customs for weeks.

OSTRICH

You about to be more so. While man was away? Theyall talking about Dott. How he got control over Time.

BILLY

No such thing.

OSTRICH

Allow it. Man's dramatically cut down on man's reality intake.

BILLY

That's one way of putting it.

OSTRICH

Serious. They saying he can mess with man's head. He can take away some time. Suck it out. Like a... time-vampire.

pause

BILLY

What you think, blood?

OSTRICH

I never seen it. But I dream it. You know what I mean?

BILLY

Yeah. I think I do.

pause

BILLY (con't)

I thank the stars for you, blood. You know that? You my friend. My witness even. You my safety, bruv, and I can't -

OSTRICH

None o that here. No need. Man know.

They arrive in **Cookery**.

The rest of the INMATES are there, along with GUARDS, and DOTT, in the corner alone. The noise is jovial, people chatting, clanging pots and pans.

BILLY

Full house.

OSTRICH

It's a test.

BILLY

Cookery test?

OSTRICH

Nah man, a test for us. See if we can handle it. Last chance.

BILLY

Let's handle it then!

> BILLY and OSTRICH join in
> the class, stirring, whisking.
> There is a hum of conversa-
> tions happening all around
> them. We pick up random bits.

INMATE 1

... thirty grand is big change!

INMATE 2

Not big enough to get sprayed.

> This fades back into the hum as
> another pops out.

GUARD 1

... called Mad Filth. I didn't care much for it myself.

> Back to the hum. Another pop

INMATE 3

... I'd move on her, even if he is a lifer...

> Back to the hum. The tone
> becomes louder, harsher,
> menacing. Angry. The pops of
> conversation come faster now.

GUARD 2

... really put it on the bitch, she weren't never the same...

INMATE 4

... bottled him with a perfume bottle! Terrible waste...

GUARD 3

... got to hold them accountable!

> Suddenly it's silent, though the
> others continue to move and
> act as if they are still making
> the Hum from before. We hear
> BILLY's inner voice

BILLY V/O

Want to ram this knife into Ostrich's arm. Twist it. Grind it.
Harder.

> BILLY shakes his head.

BILLY V/O (con't)

Do it. Now. Stab him now. The blood. DO IT.

> BILLY shakes his head harder
> and we hear him Yelp in pain,
> he's burned his arm

                    BILLY V/O (con't)
Stung! Stung by a bee!

                         BILLY shakes his head again
                         and drops the knife into his
                         pan, making a loud noise.

                    GUARD
Alfreth!

                    BILLY
Just... just an insect bite sir. Sorry sir.

                         Now we hear DOTT in BILLY's
                         head

                    DOTT V/O
But I got you for a second there, didn't I, Billy Boy?

                         BILLY turns to look at DOTT
                         in the corner. DOTT smiles at
                         him, maybe a little wave.

                    DOTT (V/O)
Nearly made you do it Billy. Could'a made you stab him if I'd
wanted.

                         DOTT goes back to his cook-
                         ing. The noise resumes as if it
                         never stopped. BILLY is frozen.

                    OSTRICH
Billy? Hey man, you good?

                    BILLY
Nah. I don't think I am.

                         DOTT laughs.

DOTT (V/O)
Check your pockets Billy. Tonight. Check them.

OSTRICH
I think we passed the test. That's something.

End Scene 13

Scene 14

Night on the block. Shadows of
prison bars fall across the floor.
In the dark. one voice starts to
sing

INMATE

I want to break free
I want to break free
I want to break free from your lies
You're so self satisfied I don't need you
I've got to break free

He is joined by another voice

INMATE x 2

God knows. God knows I want to break free

But life still goes on
I can't get used to living without, living without

They are joined by a chorus of
voices

INMATES (ALL)

Living with you by my side
I don't want to live alone, hey
God knows. Got to make it on my own

Back to the duet

INMATE x 2

So baby can't you see

I've got to break free
I've got to break free

> A dim light on BILLY

BILY

I want to break free, yeah
I want, I want, I want, I want to break free

> BILLY, in agony, reaches in his
> pocket and, in disbelief, pulls
> out a letter. He sits down hard
> and unfolds it with a trembling
> hand and begins to read.

> For this next section, DOTT's
> voice is heard as the action
> happens.

> The bar shadows fade as the
> lights come up onPrison Ship
> - The Oasis. The sound of men
> singing together continues,
> maybe without words, rising
> and falling in volume like
> waves. The action is in shadow,
> there is fighting, working,
> escape attempts, all in rhythm.
> Like a dance.

DOTTV/O

The Oasis was the name of the Prison Ship. And we were
moored in an Oasis. Clever. Guarded by robots in rowboats.
Oil was smeared across the water like marmalade, making

slick rainbows and water-bound constellations. Pretty shapes in the relentless gloom. 200 of us on that ship, fighting for space. Hungry for it. Thirsting. Prometheus stole fire and was punished for eternity, but me? I stole water. And was sentenced to a lifetime onboard a ship. So clever. I needed water like I needed air. We all did. Aren't you going to ask me Billy-Boy? Where we were? You're so slow in asking so I'll tell you. Sahara Desert. The Where is important. Not the Who. Dott is not my real name of course. I stole that too. The only important thing is Where I lived. Places shape us Billy. They build us. I was a desert child, made from Sand and Dust. I was a man before I was a boy. Trapped on a ship in the desert. In an Oasis that thrived though there was no rain. The Hola Etta-luun. Means "Community of Believers". There was another term. "Ana mabsout beshuglak". I am happy with your work. Ana mabsout beshuglak, Billy Alfreth. No one else has made the effort. Apart from your Kate Thistle. Not ever, and I've got all the Time in the World. Literally. But you? You're living real time.So I'll give you this. Rinse me clean of this disease, and I will follow you to the very ends of the earth. I'll show you about Time. I love you Billy.

> The singing rises once more, and then fades along with the ship.

End Scene 14

Scene 15

Library.

> KATE is working at her desk
> while BILLY sorts the mail.

BILLY

I know about the Oasis.

KATE

Do you now.

BILLY

And I know that you know too. Decide Kate. How much you
want to tell me, and how much you won't.

> pause

KATE

I was telling you the truth when I said I was a student.

BILLY

We only have 15 minutes Miss.

KATE

No time at all.

BILLY

It's a start.

> pause. KATE sighs

KATE

In the 1940's the tribes of the Hola Ettaluun were discovered
deep in the Sahara Desert. Nomads. Warlords. Innocents, per-
verters, creators, call them what you will. All types of human life

converged. They came from everywhere. Do you know what a
Lurry is?

> BILLY shakes his head.

KATE (con't)
It's a hubbub. A jumble of voices, a babble. A throng.

BILLY
Right at home here, innit.

KATE
And it was right at home there as well.

BILLY
How do you know?

KATE
I was there.

BILLY
How - how do you mean?

KATE
Have a smoke with me Billy?

BILLY
Can't do that. I'll lose my Redband if I get caught with a burn
indoors. You know that.

KATE
Fuck the Redband. I have a full pack. Smoke one with me
now, the pack is yours.

> BILLY thinks it over for a
> moment.

BILLY

I haven't got a lighter.

> KATE produces cigarettes and
> a lighter from her pocket and
> they smoke.

BILLY (con't)

What was on the water.

KATE

I don't follow.

BILLY

Yes you do.

> pause

KATE

It was oil. Rainbows of oil.

BILLY

My god.

KATE

I don't know about god. There was a rumor that Kings could be grown in the Desert.

BILLY

Did you say Kings?

KATE

I'm getting ahead of myself. Appropriate I suppose. All right, let me start over. Everyone at the Oasis was obsessed with time. Time meant something different to all of us. Time is strange. Ha. Bloody understatement of the year!

BILLY

So what did it mean for you? Time.

KATE

It meant - needing to change my life every few years. Completely changing my life. I could absolutely murder a Gin and Tonic right about now.

BILLY

Miss. Please. Please make me make sense of all this. Don't help me. MAKE me.

pause

KATE

That pile of books needs new stickers.

BILLY

Miss?

KATE

Something to do. In case we're interrupted.

BILLY goes to the books and starts working. KATE joins him.

KATE (con't)

I had Usher's Syndrome when I a girl. Meant my eyes didn't work. Got worse quickly. It was frightening, each day getting darker and darker. I was miserable.

BILLY

I can imagine.

KATE

By the time I entered puberty it was affecting my hearing as well. Sometimes my balance. Some days were better than others, but the darkness. The Internal darkness. It was... On a good day I could go to school and do maybe half the lessons. Then the page would darken. Or the words would swim. Or I couldn't hear my name being called. On a really bad day, I couldn't hear my own voice. I wasn't -

> KATE's voice fades as the lights shift, and the Oasis ship appears again. The sound of the water slapping on the side, the roar of voices, BILLY sees it and is drawn toward it. He struggles against it, then towards it. Right before he reaches the ship, KATE grabs him and shakes him. The ship suddenly disappears and they are back in the Library.

KATE (con't)

Billy?!

BILLY

Fuck! What just happened?!

KATE

You stopped breathing. You were turning blue!

> BILLY takes several deep breaths, trying to steady himself

BILLY

Did you do that?

KATE

Do what?

BILLY

Take me there. Gah, I can still smell it! Oil and sweat and -

KATE

You were at the Oasis, weren't you. Is that what happened?!

BILLY

Fuck, feel like man run a sprint!

KATE

You were there.

BILLY

I was there. Wasn't I?

KATE

Okay. Be very clear now Billy. As clear as you want me to be with you. What exactly do you want to know.

BILLY

Were we there... together?

A flash of the Oasis again, a wave of sound.

KATE

Yes. Yes Billy. The first time we met was at the Oasis.

BILLY

I want to go back to my cell.

KATE

No you don't. You told me to make you understand. You want to get this, I know you do. We might not have another chance.

                         BILLY
Allow it. So. If I was there, then why...

                         KATE
...why don't you remember?

                         BILLY
Yeah. WHEN was I there?

                         KATE
My best guess? You were there, in the future.

                              A flash of the Oasis, wave of
                              sound.

                              BILLY grabs his head. Breathes
                              deep

                         BILLY
How did you get there?

                         KATE
I was 20. Mere slip of a thing, we would have said in those
days.

                         BILLY
What days.

                         KATE
1950's, 60's. I was working as a secretary in a Law Firm and -

                         BILLY
Wait a minute.

                         KATE
We haven't got a minute.

BILLY

If you were 20 in the late 1950s -

KATE

I must be a dry old bird by now? How old do I look.

BILLY

Around 35?

KATE

Close enough.

BILLY

You're chatting breeze! You can't be 20 in 1959 and only 40 in the 21st Century. It's -

KATE

For the record, I never admitted to 40.

BILLY

It's impossible.

KATE

Who says?

BILLY

Fucking nature says! It's not how it works!

KATE

It's how it works for the Hola Ettaluun. And believe me, mine is by no means the strangest of the Time Stories you could find there.

BILLY

I've never been there!

KATE

Come on Billy! You wanted it point blank. That's how I'm giving it to you. Both Barrels, Nine MM, Pow Rude-Boy! Allow it!

BILLY

You *have* been at the gin.

KATE

Nah, just drunk on excitement. Sorry, I can imagine how
strange this must be for you. But ask yourself this - what pos-
sible advantage have I got in lying?

BILLY

None.

KATE

So. Shall I resume?

pause

BILLY

Resume.

KATE

My first six months at the firm were a living hell. But it was a
living. And little by little, I earned their respect. Picked up speed
typing, come in early, stay late. I learned shorthand, so I started
sitting in on meetings and taking minutes. You wouldn't believe
some of what I heard. The divorce. Arguments. The violence.
And then I heard a...rather particular story. Me, in that office,
with my pen and my little notebook, writing Nightmare Music as
fast as I could.

BILLY

Nightmare Music.

KATE

One of the partners said my shorthand symbols looked like musical notes. I was writing symphonies, but it was Nightmare Music. I've never forgotten that.

BILLY

Man do I get Nightmare Music. The singing of the dead.

KATE

The Dead were a good band.

BILLY

I'm serious. Ever since Dott arrived. Nightmare Music.

KATE

Anyway. This man was giving his deposition and I'm thinking, "this isn't for us. You don't need a solicitor, you need a headshrinker! You're nuts!"He was talking about a Pilgrimage he's made. Didn't go quite as he'd hoped. Wanted to know if we could help him sue a place.

BILLY

A place?

KATE

He was a travel writer. Got tired of Venice and Vienna, wanted to go a bit further off the beaten track. Like, say, the Sahara? His editor wasn't champing at the bit, so this bloke offers to fund the trip himself. He heads East, searching for something he's only heard about in gossip and rumor.

BILLY

What did he want?

KATE

To find out if there really is a place on earth where "Time has stood still". Literally.

BILLY

And?

KATE

There isn't. Or if there is, it's not the Oasis. Time doesn't stand still there. That's way too simple. Time there is... like an unfelt storm. You think you're in the eye of the hurricane but actually the quiet part is where the forces rage and infect worst of all.

BILLY

Infect?

KATE

Everyone in their own way.

pause

BILLY

You alright?

KATE

There were children there Billy. Babies even. Shriveled up like walnuts. They looked 80 if they were a day. Teenagers, growing at different speeds, their torsos twice as long as their legs.

BILLY

Christ.

KATE

You get the picture?

BILLY

A freak show. Any radiation thereabout, or -

KATE

Don't belittle this. When you've seen a girls of 10 who looked pregnant with a baby that hadn't even been conceived, mate, it's no laughing matter. There was one woman, looked about 40, but she was 90 years old.

BILLY

Like you.

KATE

But more like Dott. Moving backwards through time. Born at whatever age, like when he soothed your bee-stings, and growing younger. Disappearing. Back into the egg. I'm different. I'm still going in the right direction, only slowly.

BILLY

And why was the writer suing?

KATE

He was frozen. In time. He wasn't aging at all.

End Scene 15

Scene 16

The Prison Yard.

Inmates are exercising with
weights, some playing basket-
ball, the sounds are normal;
clanking, bouncing, squeaking.
BILLY enters, sees OSTRICH
at the hoop, he joins him and
they start shooting together.

BILLY

Wogwan Ostrich.

OSTRICH

Wogwan Billy. I have news.

BILLY

What's that.

OSTRICH

Man going up, blood. Big Man Jail.

BILLY

Shut up!

OSTRICH

It's true Rudeboy. They told man right before dinner. Going
out tomorrow.

BILLY

I'll miss you Man.

OSTRICH

Ay. You hear about Bachelor?

BILLY

That yoot from Puppydog?

OSTRICH

The very same. Got twisted up while we was on gardening detail. Man was acting weird. Talk about hearing Voices. Seeing things. Talking about that Dott.

BILLY

Like what.

OSTRICH

Say man got some kinda Mind Control Voodoo shit going on. Made the yoot scratch up his own fucking arm. Voice in his head.

BILLY

Likely did it himself.

OSTRICH

Yeah. Thing is though, I never noticed no marks on him before. But this morning? Left arm look like a roadmap. Sliced to ribbons. And then, while we was weeding, the fucker picks him a yellow rose from the bed by the pool, starts to cut himself up on the thorns. Right there, in front of everyone!

BILLY

Crazy.

> Through this exchange, the clanking of the weights and the bouncing of the balls fall into a rhythm. Clank and bounce

> and squeak are all synched.
> Boom. Boom. Boom. They
> continue for a moment, trance-
> like. Finally, BILLY notices and
> flings his ball away, breaking
> the rhythm. This snaps the oth-
> ers out of it, and the noise goes
> back to normal.

OSTRICH

Thing is.

> pause

BILLY

What man?

OSTRICH

Thing is, I know what he's talking about. The voices. Maybe they putting something in the water.

> A flash of the Oasis and
> DOTT's voice

DOTT V/O

I stole water.

BILLY

How do you mean?

OSTRICH

What better way of keeping us under control.

BILLY

It's an interesting theory.

> A GUARD calls from offstage

GUARD V/O

That's it Lads, times up. Hit the showers!

OSTRICH

Already?! Can't believe how fast that hour went.

BILLY

Allow it.

OSTRICH

This whole month has gone full-pelt, bruv. Hey. You sleeping a lot more these days?

BILLY

Nah man, the opposite. Can't keep down.

OSTRICH

Telling you Man. Something in the water. Can't wait to get out of this place.

BILLY

Thanks Man. I hope I never see you again either.

OSTRICH

You won't Billy. You've been a good friend to me. Never say it, but it's so. Go legit man. Keep your nose clean. Keep the knives in the kitchen drawers, ok? Freedom is a powerful drug, no known cure. Man gonna do man's time. Play the game and keep my head down. No more dreams. Desert dreams. They grow Kings in the Desert. You were a King. O my days, I need to get out of this. I'll try not to forget you Billy, but things already fading away. Man have to get out of this place.

End Scene 16

Scene 17

Cookery class.

Everyone working nicely,
general good will. BILLY and
DOTT share a station

BILLY

So that's what Miss Thistle told me.

DOTT

Well. Now you know. Question is, what are you going to do
about it? Knowledge is -

GUARD approaches

GUARD

What's this now? Fucking sewing circle? Thought you two
couldn't stand each other.

DOTT

I don't remember saying we couldn't stand each other. Sir.

GUARD

You won't remember anything if you don't get a pissing move
on. Do your pots in the next ten minutes. Lesson's nearly
over.

BILLY and DOTT are in their
heads

BILLY V/O

The lesson is nearly over.

DOTT laughs

GUARD

The fuck is funny?

DOTT

Nothing is funny, sir.

DOTT V/O

Maybe I should have him bash his own head in with a rolling pin.

BILLY V/O

Don't even try it, you waste.

GUARD

The fuck are you on, boy?

DOTT

We was just chatting shit. We'll get the washing-up done sir.

GUARD

See that you do, son.

GUARD walks away.

DOTT

Silly fat fuck. He has no idea, has he Billy?

BILLY

Of what?

DOTT

Of what I could make him do.

BILLY

Did I meet you there, blood? What's my place? Tell me.

DOTT

Your place in the world. Ah, wouldn't we all like to know that.

pause

BILLY

Are you - you're scared. Aren't you. You don't look it, granted
that, but you are. You're getting younger. You're disappearing. You said it yourself, you thought you could stop the flow.
Back to being an infant. Thought you could do it by being
kind, generous. That's why you soothed my sting, you didn't
want to reverse. You didn't want to be a child.

DOTT

It was you who was being a child!

BILLY

I WAS a child!

DOTT

You were seven years old, and scared of a little bee.

BILLY

Whatever Dott. I'm right though. Aren't I? When did you
realize it wasn't kindness that would keep you anchored? That
you needed to exercise the black muscles in your warped little
soul in order to survive. Keep your age going north instead of
south. Am I fucking right?

DOTT

Spot on with sugar and cream.

BILLY

And you're something to do with the silences too, aren't you?
This place has gotten too quiet sometimes. It's you, right?

DOTT

You're two for two Billy boy. See, I'm just helping some of you
wacky kids to pass the time faster.

DOTT V/O

I'm TAKING TIME.

BILLY

What's in it for you?

DOTT

Just a hobby.

BILLY

Bullshit!

GUARD

Alfreth! If you two start up again it's the fucking block for
both of you!

BILLY

We're cool, Gov.

GUARD

See that you are. Clean up. Now.

>BILLY and DOTT gather their
>cooking things and start to
>clean up

BILLY

You're saving up. Right?

DOTT

Billy! That's such a nice way to put it!

BILLY

If it's true - if it's true you can steal time from us -

DOTT

I feel I'm doing you a favor!

BILLY

I've got to say, we've a lot of us been sleeping quite a bit lately.
If it's true, you're not doing it to be nice. Are you. Nice don't

work. Not for you. With nice, you're still going backward. With nice, you're dying. So this way, you - you get something back?

DOTT

You don't lie.

BILLY

You're collecting it.

DOTT

What did Ostrich say before he left. About his dreams. About Kings.

BILLY

They can be grown in the Desert. Are you one?

DOTT

Not me Billy boy. It's you.

DOTT V/O

Me, I was no more than your gardener.

End Scene 17

Scene 18

Library.

KATE and BILLY working

KATE

What's the hullabaloo this morning?

BILLY

Four yoots on A wing started a riot.

KATE

How exciting! Anything in particular?

BILLY

I could say, random cuntishness. That's what it normally is.

KATE

Not this time though? Bad food? Cell spins?

BILLY

You're learning the lingo Miss!

KATE

Thanks to you!

BILLY

But no. It's Dott. He's taking.

KATE

Taking.

BILLY

Taking back part of his... investment. He's put quite a bit in
the kitty. Now it's payback time. Ha! Literally. Pay. Back. Time.

KATE

Clever. But what does it mean?

BILLY

Best I can figure, he's buying Time. Well, trading really. What he gives, like making yoot's time go quick, he fucking takes back to save himself. Violence keeps him anchored at the right age. He doesn't want to slip backwards, so he needs to trade some damage.

KATE

What was the damage this morning?

BILLY

One ear-split, a nose-split, one hospitalization. And a left eye.

KATE

That should keep him going for a bit.

BILLY

He wants to die.

> KATE puts a gentle hand on
> his face.

KATE

We don't have long. I want to explain the rest of what I know. Ok?

BILLY

Please.

KATE

I went to the Oasis to heal my eyes. Time heals all wounds, all that. Some of the things I saw there, well, nothing could have prepared me - anyway. Now don't forget, for most people there, the Oasis was their home. So, I started to ask around. Where should I go? What part of the Oasis did I need to cure myself. Sometimes I got stories, almost fables, about people and their differing results. One day, I heard the story of Noor Aljarhalifaro - the gentleman thief. The One Who Stole The Water. Yep, that's Dott. The only thing of value in the entire place was water, and of course, that's what he stole. He was legend, I became obsessed. So, years earlier when he was older, he had a wet-nurse named Saira. They grew to be friends. They helped each other. She was the wise woman in the township, and it was believed that it was she who gave Noor the idea of making a Pilgrimage into the desert. The idea was that deeper into the desert there were other Oases, and there, Kings could be grown from the earth. They just need special water, and faith. Saira could provide the water, bless to make it holy, if Noor had faith enough to venture into the sun and return with a King on his side. Noor heard about a boy who found grass growing deep in the desert, and he thought that might be the place. The spot where he would find soil fit to cultivate a King. Saira didn't believe the story, wanted him to wait, and she refused to bless the water. Noor did the unthinkable. He stole the water, beat Saira unconscious, and set out into the wilds. For months, rumors flew. "He's out there, growing roses. Roses in the desert. They are knitting together to grow a king". One year later, Noor returned, expecting a Hero's welcome. But the crime of water theft was heinous. Not to mention what he had done to poor Saira. So rather than celebrate his return, he was stripped, shackled, and sentenced to Life aboard the Prison Ship. Life, as you know by now, having many meanings there. And as he was dragged away, they say he screamed "My King will find me! He told me he would be Everywhere!"

BILLY

Quite a town.

KATE

It was more of a world than a town. What if the Oasis was a
World before ours? What if you weren't dead before he made
you with the Rose, what if you were just... Potential. What if
he HAD to find you in order to get himself back, even if Back
is just a state of mind. Yes, the desert is a real place, I was
there, alive and well. Can I honestly say that was the same for
everyone I met there? Who knows how many others are only
dreaming of existence. Waiting to be born, somewhere in this
world or another.

BILLY

It sounds like Hell.

KATE

There's no Hell. The Oasis is half wood and half memory.
Half water and half notion. Something came to me last night.
After all this time. I wonder how many other Dotts there are
running around.

BILLY

My god.

KATE

It can't just be our Dott. Others must have gotten out. Perhaps most of them just don't spend nearly as long being a
nomad, searching country to country, trying to find an equiva-
lent of you. They live with their lot.

BILLY

With disappointment?

KATE

Like the rest of us.

BILLY

How did you know me? There. How did you know-

KATE

I was at the water when you came out of the desert. The water where I fixed my eyes. You were the first clear thing I saw, and I knew you straight away. As if I've always known you. Thank you for finding me again.

End Scene 18

Scene 19

Yard.

DOTT and BILLY are exer-
cising, other INMATES and
GUARDS are there

DOTT

What do I have to do around here to get beaten up properly?
Those pansies hardly scratched me.

BILLY

Why would you want to get beat?

DOTT

Exercise.

BILLY

Seriously.

DOTT

I am serious. Keep in shape. I made them do it.

BILLY

Does it count toward your bad shit quota?

DOTT

It certainly does Billy. I earned myself about two minutes.
Hardly seems worth it, they weren't as vicious as I had hoped.

BILLY

So what is this Dott? Blind devotion? I don't know what you
expect me to do.

DOTT

I gave you life. I grew you in the desert, against every odd
there is.

BILLY

If you say so.

DOTT

And I saved you from the bee-stings too.

BILLY

Which you said was a mistake. But okay. If you say so.

Inside BILLY's head

DOTT V/O

What do you mean IF I SAY SO?

BILLY

Don't yell.

DOTT speaks

DOTT

Don't you believe me yet?

BILLY

I believe you because I don't have any choice. But why don't I
remember?

DOTT

Because you were dead.

BILLY

Dammit Dott, what do you WANT from me??

                    DOTT
I want you to help me get back.

                    BILLY
Oh sure, I'll lend you my passport.

                    DOTT
If you go, I can follow.

                    BILLY
I'm in the same prison as you!

                    DOTT
You were dead then. You can be dead again.

                    BILLY
Is that a threat?

                    DOTT
Quite the opposite. I'm offering you a gift.

                              Other INMATES join them
                              and a game of basketball starts.
                              The conversation continues in
                              BILLY's head

                    BILLY V/O
What do you mean by dead?

                    DOTT V/O
Can't you see the end is in sight?

                    BILLY V/O
No.

                    DOTT V/O
You came to see me on the ship.

BILLY V/O

No!

DOTT V/O

I will find you or you will find me. That's what you said. And I
have found you. You helped me escape from the ship, and for
that I'm grateful. Eternally. Now I can help you escape from
this prison.

BILLY V/O

No one has ever escaped from Dellacort.

DOTT V/O

Open your mind.

BILLY V/O

I can't think with you in here!

> DOTT stops playing and stares
> at the other INMATES. They
> freeze for a moment, and then,
> with sad looks on their faces,
> begin to fight each other. A
> GUARD runs in and breaks
> them apart.

GUARD

The fuck is going on here!

INMATE

I... I don't know sir.

> GUARD turns to DOTT

GUARD

You involved in this?

DOTT

Sir?

GUARD

So help me Dott...All right you two, move along, quick as you can.

>GUARD grabs the INMATES
>and drags them off

DOTT

You were saying?

BILLY

How can we escape? You going to steal more time from me?

DOTT

A mere demonstration.

BILLY

How did I help you off the ship?

DOTT

You repaid my gift of life.

BILLY

The rose. You grew me.

DOTT

A drop of water, day by day for a million days. I wished you alive. It was faith.

BILLY

But not reason.

DOTT

You know who you are. You just can't see the whole picture yet. But you found me.

BILLY

Wait, you came here. You found me.

DOTT

No. You were born. I was waiting for you to arrive. I prayed for your mother. I watched you grow. I convinced your father to leave, you didn't need him. I -

BILLY

What??

DOTT

He was a violent man. I couldn't risk him hurting you. It wasn't hard, he all but had his hat and coat on anyway.

BILLY

What did you do?

DOTT

Paid him. See, I thought then that if I was kind and good I'd be able to get older. I was scared of getting young, going through that horror again.

BILLY

Again?

DOTT

It's not my first time around the block. Every time I go around it's different, but it's always full of terror and angst.

BILLY

How old are you, all together?

DOTT

I don't know. Maybe I was there for 2000 years before I was dragged out of the desert. 2000 has a nice ring.

BILLY

Are you saying - are you Christ?

DOTT

Would you like to pray to me?

BILLY

Is that - is that how you find the people to use? By answering prayers?!

DOTT

What do you think, you daft bastard! Did Christ beat joggers by the side of the canals? If so, it certainly puts a different spin on things! Talk about a Last Supper! Macaroni cheese and pudding.

The GUARD enters

GUARD

You two, back to your Wings. Won't tell you twice, move along now.

GUARD grabs DOTT and leads him off.

DOTT

Miss you already Billy!

GUARD

Shut up!

Lights shift to BILLY's head.

BILLY V/O

How many times can you think a thought without wearing it out? But I can't see the answer yet. Are we linked? Our energy? If Dott dies, what happens to me? I don't remember yet, but I will.

End Scene 19

Scene 20

Cell block.

> Like earlier, one voice sings

INMATE

I want to break free
I want to break free
I want to break free from your lies
You're so self satisfied I don't need you
I've got to break free

> He is joined by another voice

INMATE x 2

God knows. God knows I want to break -

> An alarm is heard, and flash-
> ing emergency lights start. The
> flashing light should be slow
> enough to illuminate pictures
> of a riot. Screams are heard,
> and wild gibberish, along with
> GUARDS' voice and Radio
> calls.

BILLY

Dott?! Dott! Is this you?!

> DOTT's voice answers him

DOTT V/O

Tonight is the night. Don't worry, you're asleep. I'll take this time away from you. You won't need to see a thing.

BILLY

I want to see a thing! I've been waiting so long!

DOTT V/O

As you like it. Wake up then Billy. The show must go on!

BILLY

Do it!

> In a counter point to the lights, a slow deep, drum noise rises, almost a heartbeat. All the inmates are pounding their heads against their walls in unison, keeping time. Blood starts to run down faces. A fire breaks out in a cell. Steam from another. GUARDS try to manage the chaos.

> The Prison fades out as the Oasis Ship fades up. The beat shifts and becomes the sound of one big drum, and a GUARD acting as Coxswain calls to the INMATES

GUARD

Pull! Pull! Pull!

> The GUARD is walking up and down the row of INMATES, he carries a whip on his hip and is beating the drum to keep them

in time. DOTT sits among the
INMATES.

BILLY steps onto the ship, in
front of the GUARD.

GUARD

What do you think you're doing?

BILLY

Change of leadership.

GUARD

Oh you think so?

BILLY

I know so.

BILLY pulls out a small knife.

GUARD

Stay where you are.

BILLY

Let them go!

GUARD

You know I can't do that.

BILLY

We'll take our chances on the water.

GUARD

In the oil? Impossible. No one survives the oil.

BILLY

How many have tried?

GUARD

A good many. Now drop the knife and rest. I assure you an easy shift when it's your turn to row again.

BILLY

Ha! My back still stings from yesterday's flogging.

GUARD

Not by my hand.

BILLY

It doesn't matter who's hand. This ends now.

> GUARD slowly takes out his whip and cracks it close to BILLY, who jumps back.

GUARD

That was a warning. Now stand aside!

BILLY

No.

> The thin rope of the whip is still on the floor, and BILLY quickly steps on it. GUARD tries to pull it back, and BILLY walks along the rope toward him. BILLY stabs the GUARD in the arm with the knife. GUARD screams and pulls the whip hard. BILLY is knocked off and they begin to fight. The INMATES watch in silence. After a moment, BILLY stabs the GUARD, who collapses.

BILLY

You're all free! Go!

> The INMATES are still silent.
> Motionless. Slowly, DOTT
> stands.

BILLY (con't)

You can be free.

> GUARD suddenly sits up, pulls
> the knife out and screams for
> help.

BILLY (con't)

Run!!

> DOTT freezes for a moment,
> then runs off. two more
> GUARDS enter, grab BILLY
> and begin to beat him. A
> SPLASH as DOTT jumps
> overboard. The three GUARDS
> continue their beating.

> BILLY's head-

BILLY V/O

Three men! Beaten by Three Men.

> Aloud -

BILLY

What's in it for me, Dott? What's in this for me??

> Lights shift back to the Prison
> Cell ward. The sound of the

riot rises again, and the emergency lights flash. They are joined by police lights outside, red and blue swirls. INMATES are screaming, laughing, bloody, ragged. GUARDS try to manage the riot but they are overwhelmed. BILLY climbs to the top of the bars in his cell.

The noise fads as the lights shift back to the Oasis. BILLY climbs down a rope or ladder and lands on the beach. He sees a figure in a black hooded robe waiting for him. BILLY walks slowly towards him and the figure removes his hood. It is DOTT.

DOTT

Welcome back.

BILLY

Water. I need water.

DOTT

Don't we all.

DOTT hands BILLY a water skin and he drinks deeply.

DOTT (con't)

Hurry. We have to go.

                    BILLY

Where are we going?

                    DOTT

You know where.

                    BILLY

The desert.

                    DOTT

That's right.

                    BILLY

Am I dead again?

                    DOTT

Only if you want to be. Fuck Billy! You drank the whole thing!

                    BILLY

That's King Billy to you.

                    DOTT

There's no time. Let's go!

                    BILLY

What's the hurry for fuck's sake?

                    DOTT

It will be night soon.

                    BILLY

How far are we going?

                    DOTT stops and grabs BILLY.

                    DOTT

What did you leave behind?

BILLY

Chaos. Utter chaos. You really stuck it to them, Dott, I'll give you that.

DOTT smiles

DOTT

I knew it! Can you feel it Billy? It's working. I'm getting older! Time is catching up! Come on, let's get to the roses.

BILLY

You want us to walk through the desert for two weeks?!

DOTT

Billy. It was enough. What I did in the prison, it was enough! Time is behind us, pushing us to the roses. It's shoving us! Like riding a wave. Do you surf?

BILLY

No!

DOTT

Well, it's never too late to learn a new skill!

> Suddenly BILLY and DOTT seem to fly over the desert, zipping past dunes and cacti. DOTT laughs and calls to BILLY as they fly

DOTT

This is it! This is the harvest!

BILLY

You sold your soul for one trip backwards.

DOTT

Who says I ever had a soul Billy!

> The scenery changes from
> bleak desert to an actual Oasis.
> Verdant, green, with wildly
> growing rosebushes every-
> where. As quickly as it began,
> their flight stops. They fall to
> the ground, breathing heavily.

BILLY

You need to get yourself a gardener.

DOTT

Isn't it stunning.

BILLY

Not exactly the Garden of Eden.

DOTT

I never said it was Eden.

> DOTT sees one single white
> rose, growing alone. He sits in
> front of it.

DOTT

This is it.

BILLY

I come from that?!

DOTT

Come closer Billy, sit with me.

BILLY sits. He reaches his hand toward the rose, and pricks himself on a thorn. There is blood.

BILLY

Ow!

DOTT

Yes Billy. Yes. It's time.

DOTT pulls his hood up and starts to sway. Slowly, the sound of the drumming rises again, matching his rhythm. The scenery shifts from images of the Prison Riot, to the Prison Ship, to Desert, to Rose Garden. BILLY watches it all as DOTT continues to sway. The drum beats faster and DOTT's hood falls away. He is older. The scenery shows images of violence, boys fighting, people screaming silently, war, Dellacotte prison. DOTT turns to BILLY.

DOTT

Be strong Billy.

BILLY

Don't do this!

DOTT

Too late. Can't you see? It was always too late.

>DOTT collapses to the ground.
The lights fade. Blackout.

End Scene 20

Scene 21

Hospital.

BILLY is in a hospital bed, one leg shackled to the bed. He wakes up suddenly, with a start. He has a streak of white in his hair.

BILLY

Water!

KATE comes in with water.

KATE

Here you go, son. Just a sip.

BILLY

Where am I?

KATE

Hospital.

BILLY

The town?!

KATE

The hospital. You inhaled a lot of smoke.

BILLY

How's Dott?

KATE

Who?

BILLY

Ronald Dott?

KATE

There have been a lot of you boys in here this morning. All hands on deck for us, I volunteered to come help.

BILLY

Kate?

KATE

You can call me Miss Thistle, Mr. -

>   She looks at a chart on his bed.

KATE (con't)

Alfreth.

>   pause

BILLY

Allow it.

KATE

I think that's my favorite of all the slang. Allow it. Can you tell me, what started the riot? No one seems to have an answer.

BILLY

It's about time.

KATE

Well. You rest. You should be free to go back to Dellacorte soon, see this red check on your chart? Means there's nothing seriously wrong with you. Your hair - has it always had that streak of silver?

BILLY

Silver?

> KATE takes a compact from
> her pocket and shows him in
> the mirror.

BILLY (con't)

Ay Miss. I was made that way.

KATE

Quite unusual.

BILLY

Any screws here?

KATE

Guards? One or two. They say they've never seen a late shift like this one. Full scale riot. All the beds are full, corridors too. Guards and Inmates alike. I shouldn't say this, but it could be Time Bomb. Not enough Guards to look after all of you. And the Prison is a disaster. You lot will be cleaning for some time I hear.

BILLY

What's going to happen to us, do you know?

KATE

I'm sure you can guess. Lockdown. Goodness only knows how long. No games, no TV. They've shut off the hot water too, though you didn't hear that from me. If there's nothing else Mr. Alfreth, I have to check on the rest of the -

BILLY

Miss! Wait. Please. What about Dott?

KATE

I'm sorry, I don't know that name. I work in the Library, I saw many Inmate's names, but that one isn't ringing a bell with me. Good luck Mr. Alfreth. I hope you find your friend.

> KATE starts to leave, turns at the door and locks eyes with BILLY for a moment. She smiles gently at him, and goes.
>
> In BILLY's head -

BILLY V/O

Dott? Hit me back? Dott? Well. I hope it worked. I hope I helped you back. I was your passport. Or did I - how many memories do we cheat ourselves on? Like colors, how do we know that my blue isn't another man's gold. Maybe my blue is Kate's gold now. Who knows. There's nothing I can do about it now, just do my Time. She can find me if she wants me. I've got plenty of Time to exhaust.

End Play

www.ingramcontent.com/pod-product-compliance
Lightning Source LLC
Chambersburg PA
CBHW032003080426
42735CB00007B/494